WALRUSES

THE SEA MAMMAL DISCOVERY LIBRARY

Sarah Palmer

Rourke Enterprises, Inc.
Vero Beach, Florida 32964

Library of Congress Cataloging-in-Publication Data

Palmer, Sarah, 1955-
  Walruses.

  (The Sea mammal discovery library)
  Includes index.
  Summary: Describes, in simple terms, the
appearance, infancy, habits, behavior, and
habitat of the walrus.
  1. Walruses—Juvenile literature. [1. Walruses]
I. Title.
II. Series: Palmer, Sarah, 1955-
Sea mammal discovery library.
QL737.P62P34 1989   599.74'7   88-26429
ISBN 0-86592-358-2

Printed in the USA

TABLE OF CONTENTS

WALRUSES

The scientific group name for walruses, seals, and sea lions is *Pinniped*. The largest and strongest *Pinnipeds* are the walruses (*Odobenus rosmarus*). There are two **species** of walruses: the Atlantic and the Pacific. These two species are very similar. Atlantic walruses are a little smaller than Pacific walruses.

Pacific walruses are larger than Atlantic walruses

HOW THEY LOOK

The most noticeable things about walruses are their stubby whiskers and their sharp tusks. Walruses are one and a half times the size of sea lions. They can grow as long as twelve feet and weigh nearly one and a half tons. One-third of a walrus's weight is made up of **blubber**, or fat.

Walruses have whiskers and large tusks

WHERE THEY LIVE

Walruses live in the cold regions of the North Pole. They are found in the **pack ice** that floats in shallow shellfish beds. In the summer, when there is no ice farther south, walruses stay mainly within the Arctic Circle. When the ice creeps southwards in the winter months the walruses move with it. Pacific walruses **migrate** through the Chukchi Sea and the Bering Straits to spend the winter in the Bering Sea.

Walruses live in the frozen Arctic areas

WHAT THEY EAT

Walruses eat about six percent of their body weight in food each day. That means that a one-ton walrus needs 120 pounds of fish and shellfish each day! Walruses dive down to the ocean bottom to feed on clams and other shellfish. People used to think they ate the clams by digging them with their tusks. Scientists no longer believe that. They think walruses simply suck the clams from their shells.

Walruses suck shellfish from the rocky shallows

Enormous herds of walruses haul out to rest on the rocks

Walruses sometimes fight each other

THEIR TUSKS

Both male and female walruses have tusks. The tusks are really extra long teeth that grow from either side of the walrus's top jaw. They are made of a kind of bone called **ivory**. Eskimos sometimes carve walrus tusks into tools and ornaments. The tusks begin to grow when the walrus is about four months old. They keep growing as long as the walrus is alive. A walrus's tusk can measure over three feet and weigh ten pounds.

Walruses' tusks can grow very long

LIVING IN THE OCEAN

In spite of their bulk, walruses swim strongly and with great ease. Walruses have huge, triangular hind, or back, **flippers** about three feet across. By kicking their hind flippers, walruses push their bodies through the water. Their smaller fore, or front flippers are used for steering. Walruses usually feed at depths between 30 and 150 feet. They can stay underwater for up to twelve minutes.

Walruses kick their huge back flippers to push them through the water

THEIR BODIES

Under the walruses' thick, tough skin is a three inch layer of blubber. In the Arctic's bitter chill, blood is drained from the blubber into the walruses' bodies. Away from the cold temperature outside it can be kept warm. If walruses become too hot, their blood is pumped back into the blubber where it can be cooled. The blood just under their skin makes walruses look very pink.

The skin of walruses is gray when they are
 in the water, and turns pink when they haul out to rest

BABY WALRUSES

Baby walruses are about four feet long at birth. They weigh about 130 pounds. Most **calves** are born in May. Female walruses have only one calf at a time. Often they carry their young on their backs. The calves stay with their mothers for about two years. When they are able to look after themselves, the young walruses leave their mothers to join a herd.

This young male walrus is beginning to grow tusks

THE WALRUS FAMILY

Walruses do not live in a family unit. Male and female walruses herd separately. The males form one herd. The females look after the young walruses in another herd. Walruses **haul out** onto **ice floes** and rocks to rest, usually in very large herds. Sometimes herds of several thousand walruses can be seen. The walruses crowd together, often lying on top of one another in the crush.

GLOSSARY

blubber (BLUH ber) — a thick layer of fat under the skin of a sea mammal

calves (KAV s) — baby walruses

flippers (FLI purz) — short flat limbs that help a walrus move

haul out (HALL OWT) — to rest on dry land

ice floe (ISE floe) — a large, floating chunk of ice

ivory (EYE vore ee) — a kind of bone from which a walrus's tusks are made

migrate (MI grayt) — to move from one place to another, usually at the same time each year

pack ice (PAK ise) — an area where pieces of ice float close together in the sea

species (SPEE seez) — a scientific term meaning kind or type

INDEX